The Enchantress of Numbers: The Story of Ada Lovelace

Published by Girls Rock Math

For more copies of this book, please email: info@girlsrockmathematics.com

Designed and Set by Jessica Johnson

Illustrations by Brittany Goris

Have you ever wished you could fly? Like you, Ada Lovelace was once a child, and she dreamt that she could soar like the birds.

Ada was about as lonely a child as there ever could be. She had no friends, never went to school, and rarely left the estate she called home. This wasn't her choice, however, it was just how things were.

Ada's mother and father were an odd pair. They never got along, not even when they first met. They got married nonetheless (love didn't matter much in those days) and had Ada shortly after.

Lord Byron was romantic. Lady Byron was logical. Lord Byron was an athlete and a daredevil. Lady Byron was prim and proper. Not only that, but Lord Byron was a famous poet. He loved fame and travel, and one day he left and never came back.

Lady Byron was furious that Lord Byron never came home. She made a promise to herself that she would raise Ada to be the complete opposite of her father. This meant no fun or games for Ada, and absolutely no poetry! From dawn until dusk, Ada was taught by teachers and tutors.

She was taught French, German, geography, needlework, drawing, music, dancing, Latin, Greek, algebra, mathematics, geometry, calculus, and philosophy.

Without any spare time to play, Ada looked for every opportunity to escape, even if it was only in her imagination.

One afternoon during her Greek lesson, the governess read her the myth of Daedalus and Icarus. In this myth, Daedalus and Icarus escaped from prison wearing wings of feathers and wax. Icarus flew too close to the sun, and his wings melted and he crashed to the earth.

Ada thought to herself, "How dumb! Of course wax would melt. If you wanted to fly, you'd need a machine. Machines can do anything you want them to."

In those days machines were new inventions, and people were just beginning to use them. The newest inventions were the steam locomotive and the camera. New machines were being invented all the time, and Ada was sure she could make one to help her fly.

That very night while Ada lay in her bed, she heard a strange sound. She lit a candle and saw her cat Puff munching on a bird. When she looked closely at its wing she could see the bones and tiny feathers, and she imagined how a gust of wind could carry a bird high in the sky. In a burst of inspiration, she decided she would use the God-given design of the bird wing to create wings big enough for a human. **A human flying machine**. She called her invention

Flyology.

Ada created a laboratory in their barn. She gathered books on the anatomy of birds, as well as wire, silk, and the tools she needed to begin her inventing. Ada worked tirelessly for over a year, sending her mother letters about her progress on

Flyology.

During every spare moment between her lessons, Ada worked in the laboratory doing calculations and examining the birds Puff collected in the garden.

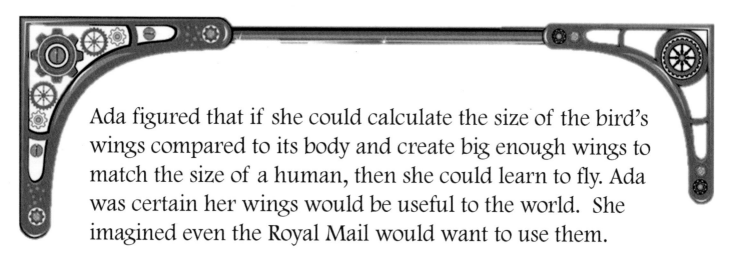

Ada figured that if she could calculate the size of the bird's wings compared to its body and create big enough wings to match the size of a human, then she could learn to fly. Ada was certain her wings would be useful to the world. She imagined even the Royal Mail would want to use them.

Lady Byron, however, was not as excited as Ada was about

Flyology.

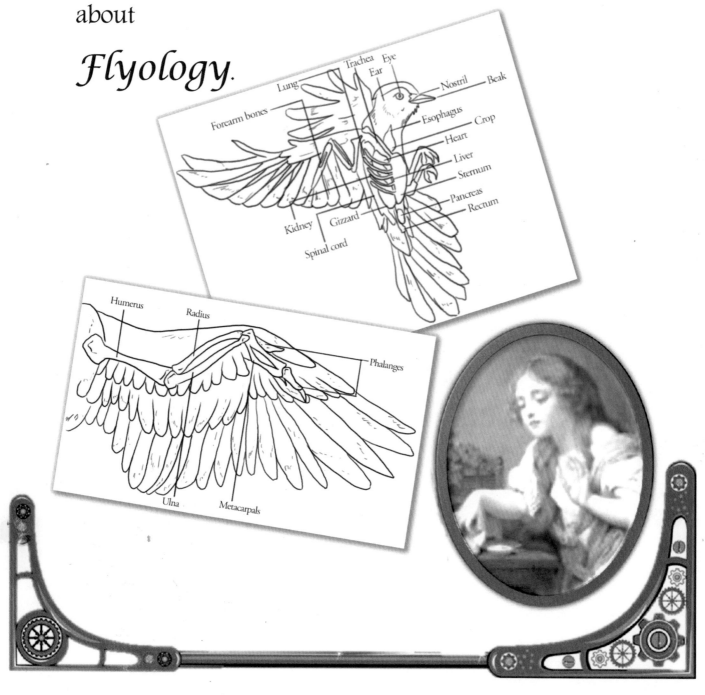

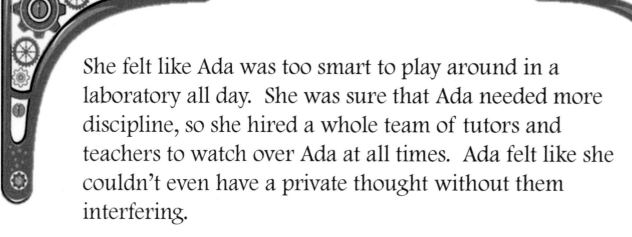

She felt like Ada was too smart to play around in a laboratory all day. She was sure that Ada needed more discipline, so she hired a whole team of tutors and teachers to watch over Ada at all times. Ada felt like she couldn't even have a private thought without them interfering.

Finally, at 18 years old, her mother
allowed her to go into the city. The first place she went
was the home of Charles Babbage, one of the most brilliant
inventers in London.

He had invented many wonderful things, such as a beautiful
silver ballerina that could be wound up to dance and spin.
When a key was turned, her arm would outstretch and flutter
and her leg would lift in the
air. Just as swiftly as she
came to life would she
freeze, when the
ticking parts inside her came to
rest.

Most girls would be fascinated by the dancer alone, but when Ada went to Babbage's home another machine caught her eye. It was the size of a steamer trunk, and was full of cogs and gears. Most of them were labeled with the numbers 0-9 across the sides.

"What is that?" asked Ada enthusiastically. The numbers fascinated her. Of all the things in the world, to Ada numbers were the most beautiful.

"Ah yes… I have spent ten years working on this. I call it the Difference Engine. It's a thinking machine. I'll demonstrate what it can do if you watch the numbers carefully."

After turning and tuning, humming and hissing, the machine started. Several minutes later the numbers began to move. Watching carefully, Ada noticed a pattern in what they were doing.

"It's arithmetic!"

"Indeed," said Mr. Babbage. "This machine will save the government millions of dollars. Every year the economy loses tons money, and hours and hours of work due to simple mathematical errors. This machine will save us from that. By the time it's done it will have 20,000 more parts, and be the size of locomotive car. If I can finish it, that is."

"I would love to help you!" Ada declared.

"My dear," Mr. Babbage said, "in order to work this machine you must know arithmetic, algebra, square numbers, and calculus. Have you been taught any mathematics?"

"Yes," Ada answered with pride. She didn't mention that she was considered a mathematical genius.

Soon after, Lady Byron decided that it was time Ada got married, now that she was an adult. She insisted Ada attend every ball, with all of the other sophisticated young people in London. Ada would go, but she refused to adhere to the strict dress code and mind her manners the way her mother wanted her to. She always spoke in a very loud voice, and talked constantly about algebra, instead of polite subjects like opera. On top of that, she would dress however she pleased.

Eventually she did meet a man: the Earl of Lovelace. He was also an inventor, and admired Ada's genius. He swore to Ada that he'd support her in all of her inventions, in her mathematics, and her work with Mr. Babbage. Ada married him right away. She did it to please her mother mostly, but she also liked him quite a bit.

Together they raised three children, although Ada felt like children made lots of noise, which interfered with her thinking!

Ada continued to work with Mr. Babbage on his machine, and they travelled all over Europe to show it off. People liked the idea of it, but no one really understood what it could do. Many didn't believe it at the time, but their ideas would one day change the world. Mr. Babbage's machines became what were used make the first computer, and Ada's ideas became the blueprint for the first computer language! Sadly, however, it would take another hundred years for the first functioning computer to be built.

This is one of the first computers in 1941. These early computers were the size of a room!

All children inherit different things from their parents. Ada had her father's dark hair and her mother's sharp nose. She had her mother's strong mind for science and mathematics, but Ada was also the daughter of a poet. She never knew her father, but she inherited some of his gifts as well. She inherited his curiosity and wonder, and his gift of writing. When Mr. Babbage needed someone who could share the idea of the "thinking machine" with the world, he asked Ada to write the book. Ada worked tirelessly on it for two years, and when it was finally published it was a big hit. She became known as the "Enchantress of Numbers." The book was a sensation, and so was Ada. She was nearly as famous as her father had been!

For people like Ada, who had grown up in a time when rooms were lit by candlelight and people traveled by horse-drawn carriage, the world had changed fast. Suddenly, gaslights were everywhere, and railways made multi-day trips into something that could be done in an afternoon. Inventions such as the steamboat, telegraph, and sewing machine were revolutionizing the world. During times that were changing so quickly, the idea that someday machines may be able to think was overwhelming, yet exciting. For people to know that a woman wrote the book explaining it, during a time when women weren't supposed to understand science or math, was one of the most revolutionary ideas of all!

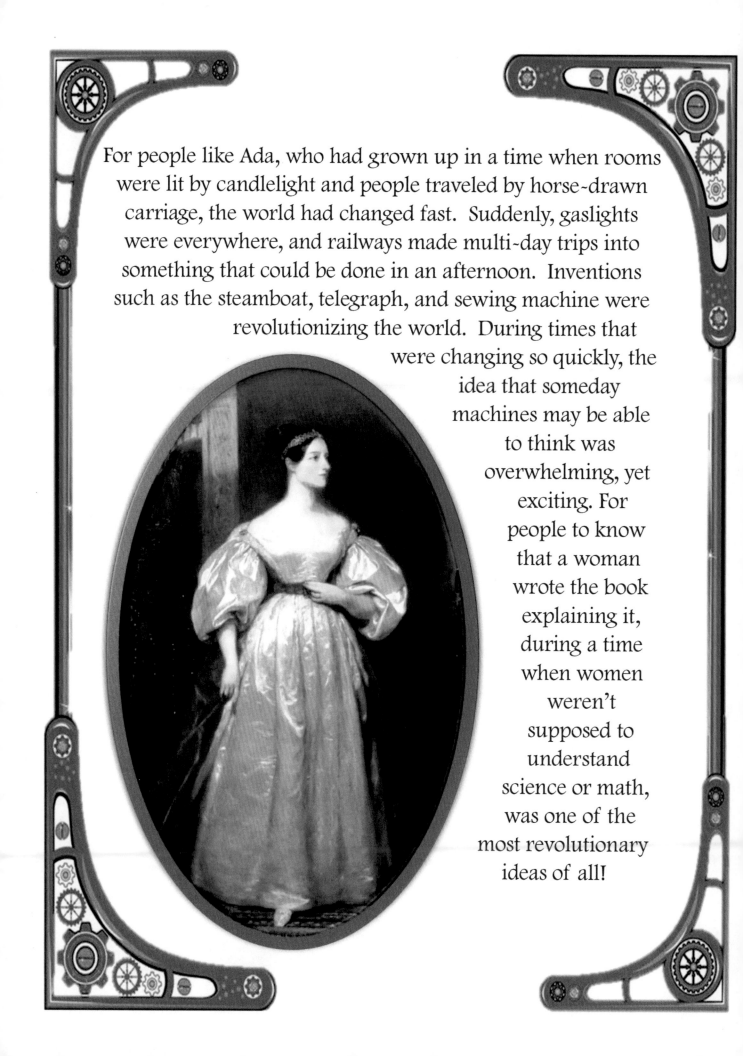

Timeline

1815: Ada Byron is born

18:16 Ada's parent separate

1824: Lord Byron dies in Greece

1827: Ada works on Flyology

1833: Ada and her tutor William try and fail to elope

1833: Ada goes to Charles Babbage's house and sees the Difference Engine

1835: Ada marries William King (Earl of Lovelace)

1836: Ada gives birth to her first child

1841: Ada begins working on the book about the Analytical Engine

1843: The book is published in England

1852: Ada dies of a stomach tumor and is buried next to her father

1939: The Complex Number Calculator is completed (Made by Bell Telephone Laboratories)

1941: The first computers are created, and used in WWII

1980: The first American computer programming language is named Ada, in honor of Ada Lovelace

Story Discussion

1. How did Ada follow her dreams? What gives someone the ability to do this?

2. What are some ways life was different for girls in Ada's time than girls today? What makes her story unusual for the time in which she was living?

Afterword

Ada Lovelace and Charles Babbage never actually built the first computer. It was just a dream. It took over 100 years for people to develop a real computer, and then 150 more before it could do the things that Ada wanted it to. She envisioned that a machine could do anything that could be programmed into it with logic, like showing words, pictures, and music—not just numbers.

Women have always been a part of computing. In the 1940s, it was women who were the first programmers, but even they had never heard of Ada Lovelace! In those days, it was very common for women to major in math in college. Grace Hopper was a Navy admiral who invented an easy to use computer programming language that made it possible for even more people to learn to code.

Today only about 1 out of every 5 computer programmers is a woman, so what happened? One theory is that it was because the ads for the first computers showed mainly men and boys using them to get boys interested in playing video games. Girls were shown on TV and in movies as being frustrated by computers and technology, or thinking they were nerdy. Big box office movies like *Revenge of the Nerds* and *Weird Science* featured geeky boys using computers to win a beautiful, popular girl's heart.

Revenge of the Nerds

Teachers would see a smart boy and direct him toward a computer. Soon, boys were learning to program for fun, and girls started to see programming computers as something either hard or just uncool. After all, the movies featured nerdy guys using computers, and most girls in those days didn't want to be considered nerds. As more boys in high school started to program for fun, they would enter college already pretty smart when it came to computers! Girls who had never used a computer before found it hard to compete with boys who were already considered "computer geniuses."

Over time, fewer and fewer girls majored in Computer Science and more and more boys found a place for themselves in the world of computers. In 1984, 37% of CS majors were girls. In 2011, it was only 17%! That's a big drop! Today, more and more girls are being encouraged to learn to code. There are all-girls programming classes and coding clubs. Software like Scratch makes it fun and easy for anyone to explore computer coding! Many girls are now self-described geeks who are happy to take on the male-dominated world and show them that girls can do ANYTHING!

Apple advertisement encouraging parents to buy a computer for their son

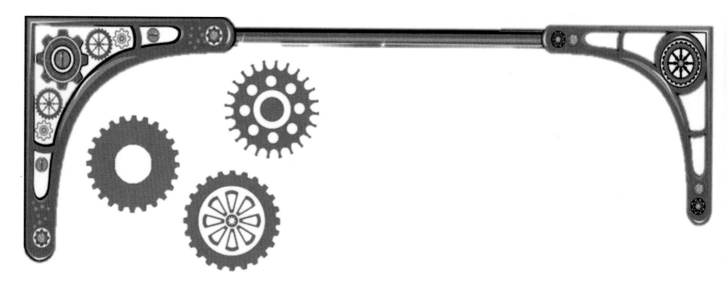

What is computer programming?

Computer programming is the art of telling a computer what do to by creating a list of instructions. Websites, games, and apps are examples of computer programs. Without a program, a computer doesn't do anything! There are different languages that computer programmers use to give these instructions. Computer programmers become experts in one or more of these languages in order to create all of the things that a computer does!

If you have ideas for games, apps, or websites, you should give computer programming a try!

Here are some great places to start:

code.org

scratch.mit.edu

playcodemonkey.com

madewithcode.com

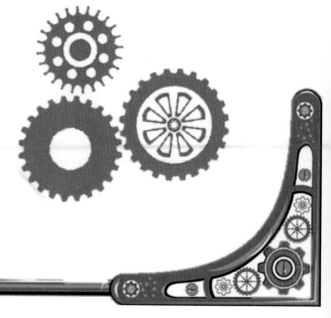

About the Author:

Jessica Christianson is a Washington native and loves living in the Pacific Northwest. She lives on Bainbridge Island with her young son, where they love to explore the local playgrounds, beaches, and hiking trails together on sunny days. Jessica, a former elementary school teacher, created the Girls Rock Math program to empower more girls to feel confident in math. Writing these books about inspiring women in the field of mathematics is one way she hopes to inspire young girls!

Made in the USA
San Bernardino, CA
02 August 2018